# ETHAN FROME

## NOTES

*including*
- *Biographical Introduction*
- *List of Characters*
- *Commentary*
- *Notes on the Major Characters*
- *Critical Notes*
- *Review Questions and Theme Top*
- *Selected Bibliography*
- *Genealogy*

*by*
*Philip E. Smith II, M.A.*
*Department of English*
*Northwestern University*

NEW EDITION

Cliffs Notes
INCORPORATED
LINCOLN, NEBRASKA 68501

| Editor | Consulting Editor |
|---|---|
| *Gary Carey, M.A.* | *James L. Roberts, Ph.D.* |
| *University of Colorado* | *Department of English* |
| | *University of Nebraska* |

ISBN 0-8220-0443-7
© Copyright 1988
by
**C. K. Hillegass**
All Rights Reserved
Printed in U.S.A.

1993 Printing

Cliffs Notes, Inc.          Lincoln, Nebraska

# CONTENTS

# Biographical Introduction

Edith Wharton was born Edith Newbold Jones on January 24, 1862, in New York City. Her family on both sides was established New York business aristocracy; her ancestry was of the best English and Dutch strains, and her favorite grandfather, Ebenezer Stevens, had been a general in the Revolutionary War. Edith Jones grew up in a brownstone mansion on West Twenty-third Street in New York. She accompanied her parents and two older brothers on trips to the country and to Europe, and from the beginning of her life she was immersed in a society noted for its manners, taste, snobbishness, and cultural vacuity. Edith Wharton reacted against this society by portraying its weaknesses in many of her novels, but from the society she absorbed strengths that made her writing powerful.

In Edith Wharton's character and her writing were evident the sense of order and tradition inherited from her society; she was respectful of the uses of art and craft, and she had a repugnance for the intrusion of the uncultured or ugly into a cultured or refined environment. At the same time she had a great respect for the power of education to make one fit to live an ordered life, and she had quite enough perspective to be able to satirize the often shallow, often stodgy and static, society which she came from. Near the end of her life, finding herself in a generation which did not understand or sympathize with her past, she began to see the society of her origin as a better and more ordered time than the economic and social seesaw of the late twenties and early thirties.

Edith Jones did not attend school; her education was accomplished through the efforts of tutors and governesses. She became proficient in French, German, and Italian and read solid literature rather than frivolous romances. Fascinated with stories, she began composing them herself when she was a small child; she called the process "making-up" and it served her as a challenging and quiet amusement in an age when children were supposed to be "seen and not heard." Edith grew up to be a very shy young lady who would rather read in her father's library than be involved in the whirl of courting. She was a reluctant debutante, but she gradually became accustomed to her role in the social life of the day.

In April, 1885, when she was twenty-three, she married Edward Wharton of Boston. He was thirteen years older than she, and he supported his new wife on his inherited income, which made it possible for the couple to live in New York and in Newport and to travel to Europe. Eventually the Newport home was replaced by one in Lenox, Massachusetts, where Edith Wharton gathered the impressions of countryside and character which formed the basis of *Ethan Frome*. The marriage lasted twenty-eight years: Edward and Edith were divorced in 1913. The first years were very happy for both partners — they lived an expensive life in Europe and America. But events began to cloud their marriage.

Edith had a mild nervous breakdown after her first book, *The Decoration of Houses* (in collaboration with Ogden Codman Jr., 1897) was published. The consulting physician recommended that Mrs. Wharton continue to write as a kind of therapy, and she turned to fiction with the publication of a volume of short stories, *The Greater Inclination*, in 1899. The step that she took in deciding to write stories and novels was one away from the established and accepted mode of life in New York society; writers were regarded at best as something less than acceptable and were usually visualized as dissipated bohemians.

Edith Wharton's first significant novel was *The Valley of Decision* (1902); set in eighteenth-century Italy, the novel showed Mrs. Wharton's sense of order in such an extreme that the characters seemed to be puppets who moved jerkily at every tug of the string. Mrs. Wharton tempered and proved her ability through more short stories and another novel until, in 1905, she published her first really substantial work, *The House of Mirth*, a novel about the New York society of her origin. Lily Bart, the heroine, inhabits a limbo between the established aristocracy and the brash new commercial class which slowly erodes the foundations of the older society. The novel is skillfully written and foreshadows in theme and technique the later *Ethan Frome;* Lily's ironic tragedy, like Ethan's, seems to be caused by a web of circumstances from which there is no escape.

As Edith Wharton's abilities increased, so did her reputation: she met Henry James in 1904 and remained his friend until his death. But the gathering of would-be and genuine literary personalities around Edith was no help to the solidarity of her marriage as Edward found himself more and more in the background. His health and mental stability became progressively poorer, and required increasingly prolonged theraputic trips to Europe. In 1907 the Whartons settled in Paris, and in 1910 Edward had a nervous breakdown and agreed to recuperate in a Swiss sanatorium. Despite efforts at reconciliation, the real companionship of their marriage had ended; with the approval of Edward's family Edith and Edward Wharton were divorced in 1913.

During this trying and crucial period Edith Wharton published essays and travel books, two collections of short stories, a book of verse, and four novels, *Madame de Treymes* (1907), *The Fruit of the Tree* (1907), *Ethan Frome* (1911), and *The Reef* (1912). The first and the last of these novels are "Jamesian" in tone, and deal with the clash between American and European sensibilities. The middle two novels are set in the United States; *The Fruit of the Tree* is an unsuccessful attempt to depict social problems in the textile manufacturing area of Massachusetts, but it has interesting foreshadowings of plot and theme in *Ethan Frome.* The Fruit of the Tree* has in it a crippling winter injury and a protagonist who loves (and in this story marries) his wife's nurse after the nurse kills the wife. These are not direct antecedents of the plot of *Ethan Frome,* but they are small indications that *Ethan Frome* was the result of a long current of thought and development in Edith Wharton's literary and personal life.

The story that became *Ethan Frome* was begun in the early nineteen-hundreds as an exercise in writing for a tutor Mrs.

Wharton had hired to improve her French conversation. She based the tale on her experiences of several summers' residence at the Wharton country home in Lenox, Massachusetts. The early form of the story is three chapters of straight narration in French without prologue or epilogue; Mattie and "Hart" (Ethan) know they love each other at the beginning of the story, and after "Anna's" (Zeena's) visit to town to hire a girl as Mattie's replacement, the lovers are forced to part. Waiting for the train to take her away, Hart swears to desert Anna and follow Mattie; this idea Mattie emphatically rejects, and so, ironically, the French version ends.

The French tale was put aside for a few years and when Edith Wharton approached it again, she made radical changes in structure and theme. Most obviously she added the device of a frame narrative, taken she tells us, from Browning's *The Ring and the Book* and from a short story of Balzac's, "La Grande Bretêche." Balzac's story is about a traveler who visits a small village and becomes fascinated with an old house; wishing to find out about it (as the narrator of *Ethan Frome* is made curious when he sees Ethan leaving the post office), he asks the villagers, and the story is gradually put together as a composite of different bits of information. In theme, *Ethan Frome's* vision of frustration, catastrophe, and prolonged pain and despair reflects a maturity and complexity of thought not apparent in the earlier vignette composed in French.

Serialized in *Scribner's Magazine* from August to October of 1911, *Ethan Frome* was published in book form the same year. Popular response was enthusiastic, and critics and reviewers praised the finely crafted structure as well as the bleak, naturalistic vision of New England country life. The book showed that Edith Wharton's talents were by no means limited to novels of New York society manners. Mrs. Wharton used the New England locale again in a novel, *Summer* (1917), and a short story, "The Bunner Sisters." As in *Ethan Frome* the two later efforts show the stifling effect of the environment on individuals who try without success to break away and then fall back into smothering frustration and despair.

In 1913, the year of her divorce, Edith Wharton published another novel based on the New York social milieu, *The Custom of the Country*. The very name of the heroine, Undine Spragg, suggests the unpleasant qualities of caricature that differentiate her from the earlier and more likable Lily Bart. Undine seeks only after material comfort and pleasure, and the values she represents are those which were destined to break down the aristocratic morality of the established society. Also set in the New York environment was Mrs. Wharton's Pulitzer Prize-winning novel, *The Age of Innocence* (1920), wherein Newland Archer (as does Ethan Frome) tries unsuccessfully to break the chains of societal custom and morality which restrain him from loving the woman who truly interests him. Like *Ethan Frome*, *The Age of Innocence* is a gem of stylistic control and brilliance.

With the eruption of World War I in 1914, Mrs. Wharton demonstrated her deep love of France by lending her efforts and influence to numerous efforts to care for the wounded, for refugees, and for war orphans. In *Fighting France, from Dunkerque to Belforte* (1915) she praised the French war effort and told of her visits to the troops on the various battlefronts. For her contributions to France during the war she was awarded the Legion of Honor.

After World War I, Mrs. Wharton made France her permanent residence. She contributed heavily to charity, and she liked costly homes, cars, and servants; to help pay for it all she catered to the profitable market of the women's magazines with the serialization of novels such as *The Glimpses of the Moon* (1922), *The Mother's Recompense* (1925), and *Twilight Sleep* (1927). These books do not reflect the artistic integrity of the fiction Mrs. Wharton had published up to and including *The Age of Innocence*, but her earlier work established her as a great American author; in 1923 she was awarded an honorary degree from Yale University, and in 1930 the American Academy of Arts and Letters elected her to membership.

Among the writings Mrs. Wharton published near the end of her life, three novels stand out as notable. *Hudson River*

*Bracketed* (1929) and *The Gods Arrive* (1932) deal with the problems of young writers encountering society, New York in the first book and Europe in the second. These two novels, along with *The Buccaneers* (unfinished, and published posthumously in 1938), marked a return to the carefully thought-out and well-written fiction of Mrs. Wharton's best years, and it is unfortunate that, in 1937, her death from an apoplectic stroke interrupted the finishing of her last work. Mrs. Wharton's papers were given to Yale University with the stipulation that certain of them were not to be released until 1968.

With the exception of *Ethan Frome* and a few other works, Edith Wharton's best fiction was devoted to the society that she knew best, the New York aristocracy which prepared her to meet life with a sense of order and dignity which is ever present in her writing. Students who have read only *Ethan Frome* would do well to expand their acquaintance with a truly remarkable woman by venturing into the finely crafted world of *The House of Mirth* and *The Age of Innocence*.

# List of Characters

### Ethan Frome

The protagonist (central character) of the novel; trapped by circumstances, he works his farm and sawmill to provide a living for himself and his sickly wife.

### Zenobia (Zeena) Frome (née Pierce)

Ethan's wife, who became a brooding hypochondriac after he married her.

### Mattie Silver

Zeena's sweet-tempered cousin who lives with the Fromes as a housekeeper; she understands Ethan and falls in love with him.

### The Narrator

An engineer whose work brings him to Starkfield for several weeks; he relates the "frame" story (prologue and epilogue).

### Harmon Gow

A retired stage driver and resident of Starkfield who supplies the narrator with part of the story of Ethan Frome.

### Mrs. Ned Hale (née Ruth Varnum)

A close friend of Mattie's who later becomes one of the narrator's sources.

### Andrew Hale

Owner of a construction company in Starkfield; Ethan asks him for a fifty-dollar advance on a load of lumber.

### Ned Hale

Eldest son of Andrew, who marries Ruth Varnum.

### Denis Eady

A young man who courts Mattie; he inherits his father's store and becomes a rich grocer.

### Jotham Powell

Hired helper at the Frome farm.

### Mrs. Andrew Hale

Ethan's conversation with her causes him to decide that he cannot press his application to her husband for a fifty-dollar advance.

### Widow Homan

Owner of a store in Starkfield who sells glue to Ethan.

### Martha Pierce

An aunt of Zeena's, whom she stays with on her visit to Bettsbridge.

### Dr. Buck

The doctor Zeena sees in Bettsbridge, who advises her that she has "complications" and should do no housework.

## Philura Maple

Another aunt of Zeena's, who sent the Fromes the red pickle dish as a wedding present.

## Daniel Byrne

A neighbor of the Fromes who transports Mattie's trunk to the train station.

## Mrs. Frome

Ethan's ailing mother, to care for whom he must leave college after his father's death.

# Commentary

## THE PROLOGUE

The key to an understanding of *Ethan Frome* lies not merely in knowing what happens in the novel; one must also be aware of the use of structure and style which qualifies *Ethan Frome* as one of Edith Wharton's greatest works. The structure of the novel is admirably suited to the author's purpose of depicting the tragedy of the title character. We are introduced to one of the important functions of the structure in the first sentence: the prologue is written in the first person, not that of Mrs. Wharton herself, but of a narrator she has created. He is an engineer who during his stay in Starkfield has put together the story of Ethan Frome from personal observation and from the fragments of the tale known to some of the townspeople.

The portions of the book written with the device of the narrator are the prologue and the epilogue, which are located in time some twenty years after the events of the main story. Structurally, these portions constitute a "frame" around the story itself; but this frame is far more than decoration. The prologue not only establishes the nature of theme and action, but also begins the characterization of Zeena and Ethan Frome, sets the important patterns of imagery and symbolism, and starts a tone of prose style which is continued throughout the book.

Theme and action, along with characterization, are usually the most easily approached and understood of the components which make up a novel, so it is with them that we will begin. We know from the author's Introduction that *Ethan Frome* is a tragedy and that Ethan himself is the main tragic character. Thus prepared, we are ready to study the action of the prologue: the narrator notices Ethan Frome at the post office and is struck by the spectacle of a strong man crippled by physical and mental pain and despair. Upon inquiry among the townspeople, he learns that Frome is the victim of a "smash-up." His curiosity whetted, the narrator questions Harmon Gow and Mrs. Ned Hale about Ethan's character and his disaster, but these two only partially satisfy his desire to know about the enigmatic cripple.

Owing to an epidemic of some mysterious horse-disease, however, the narrator is deprived of his normal transportation to the train, and Ethan Frome is employed as a driver. On a trip back to Starkfield with Frome, a terrible snowstorm causes Frome to give the narrator a night's shelter at the farmhouse. Here the action of the frame prologue is dramatically suspended, but the night at the Frome farm furnishes the narrator enough information to put together his "vision" of the tragedy.

The action can be simply comprehended, and we must look closer to find the delicate touches and skillful means by which Mrs. Wharton builds suspense, lays the foundations of character, and foreshadows the theme. We are first confronted with the physical description of Ethan Frome. As the narrator sees him, he constitutes the remains of a once-powerful and sensitive man, now bound and frustrated by the crippling effect of the sled crash.

But it is more than a wrecked body that intrigues the narrator, it is the look of incredible suffering and despair that he sees in an unguarded moment on Frome's face which causes him to persevere in his inquiry. From the first, then, despair and frustration are associated with Ethan Frome, and along with the narrator, we are anxious to discover the tragedy of the man's life.

We are not soon satisfied, for Mrs. Wharton is too clever an author to give more than the minimum needed to arouse our curiosity. Mrs. Ned Hale, therefore, is not much help to the narrator. She holds back and refuses to tell him what she knows of the true story. Harmon Gow's information is likewise not specific enough: all he knows is the sad history of the deaths of Ethan's parents and of Zeena's sicknesses, but he adds the intriguing comment that "most of the smart ones get away."

About Zeena Frome the narrator finds out next to nothing save that sickness plagues her life.

Because Mrs. Wharton carefully avoids any mention or reference to Mattie Silver in the prologue we may be inclined to think that Zeena was the other person involved in the smashup, and surely we think that it is Zeena's voice complaining on the other side of the unopened door at the end of this preliminary narration. Of course, it is Mattie, and one of the ironic purposes of the interrupted frame narration is to develop the characterization, action, symbolism, and imagery so that the full impact of what the narrator sees on the inside of the Frome house will have the maximum possible significance at the conclusion.

The introduction of Ethan Frome in the prologue prepares for the full revelation of his character in the action of the main story. Ethan's crippled physical appearance implies his tragic situation: he is a powerful and intelligent man frustrated from achieving his potential. Gradually, more of Ethan's character emerges, especially after the narrator has talked with Ethan during the trips to Corbury Flats. Harmon Gow's observation that Ethan was one of the "smart ones" is confirmed for the narrator through Ethan's interest in a book of popular science, and there is a parallel between Ethan and the narrator established when we find that both have been on engineering trips to Florida.

Mrs. Wharton implies that the narrator is the kind of man Ethan might have become if he had been able to get free of the bonds of his environment. Like the "resonator" or sounding board of a stringed instrument, the narrator's sensitive and scientific temperament enables him to understand and interpret for us the tragedy of Ethan Frome. The narrator learns little more about Ethan Frome, but he speculates on the basis of what he does know that Frome lives in a "depth of moral isolation." Mrs. Wharton here uses the narrator's comments to set up the important ideas of silence and isolation in combination with the effect of many winters on Ethan. "Silence" and "isolation" are key words and should be noted as they recur in the text.

Except for the hints drawn from the imagery and symbolism which we will shortly discuss, the character of Ethan Frome in the prologue is founded only on the small inferences and bits of information known to the narrator. Mrs. Wharton realized that the requirements of explaining the narrator's knowledge would be too great to be sustained in the main body of the story, and the rest of Ethan's character is therefore omnisciently revealed where there is no narrator and no need to bother with sources of characterization.

The most important use of symbolic imagery in the novel is the winter setting, which is first described in the prologue and carried on through the body of the story. Harmon Gow's assessment of Ethan Frome early in the prologue is that he has endured too many Starkfield winters. From then on in the novel, the winter presides over the tragedy in all its manifestations of snow, ice, wind, cold, darkness, and death. The narrator speculates that the winters in Ethan's past must have brought about a suppression of life and spirit.

Here Mrs. Wharton has the narrator use battle imagery to describe the way that winter conquers Starkfield. There are few references to any season but winter in the book: Ethan cannot remember his trip to Florida because it seems to be covered with snow. Only the recollection of the church picnic with Mattie brings the warmth of summer to the harsh and sterile landscape around Starkfield. The name "Starkfield" is significant as a symbolic summation of the moral landscape of the book. It implies the devastating and isolating effects of the harsh winters on the land and the men who work it; the name is symbolic as well of the stark, carefully controlled prose which Mrs. Wharton uses to tell the story.

The ravages of winter destroy both man's will to survive and the buildings he constructs to shield him from his environment. The "exanimate" remains of Ethan's sawmill are an example. The word "exanimate" is well chosen: we are more familiar with "inanimate," which simply means that something is without life or spirit; "exanimate," however, means that something has been *deprived* of life or spirit. By the simple substitution of a prefix Mrs. Wharton adds a dimension of meaning to the description and then follows it with appropriately personified descriptions of the millwheel and the sheds. The whole sawmill takes on the human characteristics of defeat and despair, and it personifies the frustrated and crippled Ethan Frome living and yet dead in his own isolated hell.

On his ride with Ethan Frome, the narrator sees more of the landscape, which suggests the debilitating effects of winter: the "starved" apple orchard which "writhes" over a hillside suggests the barren land which starves men instead of feeding them. The dead vine on the front porch of Ethan's farmhouse is emblematic of the dead and dying spirits that inhabit the house and its adjacent graveyard. And as the narrator acutely observes, the farmhouse itself "shivers" in the cold and looks "forlorn" and "lonely." After his important description of the loss of the "L" the narrator perceives that the farmhouse is symbolic of Ethan himself. Finally, the house's function as a place of confinement and isolation for the crippled Mattie is foreshadowed in Ethan's reminiscence of his mother's death there.

It is both ironic and appropriate, then, that a fierce snowstorm forces the narrator to take shelter in the isolated and lonely Frome farmhouse. The prologue may seem to move slowly, but Mrs. Wharton deftly changes from an early emphasis on the narrator's first impressions to one dramatic action, the trip in the snowstorm. The real destination of the trip, both stylistically and thematically, is the farmhouse which has within it the "clue" to the whole Frome story. Thus the breaking off of the narration just before the door is opened heightens the suspense and prepares us for the culmination of the tragedy in the epilogue, when, armed with the complete knowledge of the tale of Ethan Frome, we can fully appreciate the tableau of frustration and despair which greets the narrator when he enters the room.

It is impossible that the narrator could have gained the intimate knowledge of Ethan Frome's thoughts and emotions which are related in the main story, so Mrs. Wharton appropriately calls it a "vision" of the tragedy of Ethan Frome. The change from first-person to omniscient narration is also a matter of expediency for her, because the necessity of accounting for all the thoughts, feelings, and incidents related in the main section of the book would have made the device of the narrator a clumsy one, and would have obscured the simplicity with which the tale is related.

Such an omniscient vision allows the author to fragment Ethan's experiences and to fill in the background of his life slowly and in appropriate juxtaposition to the events that are described. At the conclusion, the resumption of the first-person narration fulfills the frame story and provides the bridge of twenty years' time to make the full realization of Ethan Frome's hell on earth come as a poignant climax to both the narrative frame and the novel itself.

## PART I: CHAPTERS 1-5

### ACTION, CHARACTERIZATION, THEME

Part one of the novel comprises chapters one through five, and in time elapsed, it consists of about twenty-four hours, from the time that Ethan picks up Mattie at the dance until the time that they retire the next evening. Part one and part two of the novel are told omnisciently and they make up the vision of the tragedy of Ethan Frome for which the first-person narrator of the prologue has prepared us.

In relation to the prologue and epilogue, the body of the novel takes place about twenty-four years earlier and describes the three and a half days before and including the smashup of the lovers while sledding. Our approach to the body of the novel will be first to discuss the action, characterization, and theme, then the imagery, symbolism, and style.

Because the action itself is simply comprehended, it may seem at first to be superfluous and only a means to facilitate characterization. But we must not be deceived, because Mrs. Wharton has carefully arranged the events she describes to build and complement all the aspects of the novel. In brief, after a year of admiration from a distance Ethan convinces himself of his love for Mattie and contrives to spend a somewhat anticlimactic evening of domestic quietude with her. Although Mattie does not make her love completely known to Ethan until the Shadow Pond scene in part two, the events of part one convince both characters that they would be happy togehter, and they thus have a basis in shared experience which works to intensify their feelings and leads to the climax of the attempted suicide.

The beginning of chapter one introduces us to the type of omniscient narration used throughout the body of the novel: Ethan Frome is the only character who is explored inside and out. While we are told what other characters do and say, Ethan is the only character whose thoughts and feelings we are told about. We are completely "inside" only Ethan; his consciousness reflects everything that happens. In chapter one, for instance, the bulk of what we find out is from Ethan's memory, and the action takes second place. But the action is nevertheless quite significant. When Ethan goes into town to walk Mattie back from the dance, he keeps to himself. Instead of entering the church to wait for her, he stealthily places himself outside a window and watches Mattie and Denis Eady during the last dance.

All that goes on in Ethan's mind while he waits alone in the cold serves to introduce us to him and to Mattie and Zeena. As he approaches the church, Ethan thinks how the cold, clear night reminds him of a physics experiment at college, and in turn, how his fragment of a college education has stimulated his awareness of the mysteries beyond external appearances. This sums up perhaps the most important aspects of Ethan's character: first, he is intelligent and sensitive in that he does not live a life of action only, but a life in which feelings and thoughts have an active place. Second, however, Ethan's thoughts and feelings are sometimes imprecise and irrational — they too often consist of illusions, half-truths, and cloudy meanings rather than clear intuitions or reasoned conclusions.

As Mrs. Wharton points out in the Introduction, Ethan is like a granite outcropping — his rough exterior is weathered and uncommunicative. Beneath the surface, however, Ethan's mind is continually active — he constantly speculates on past events, tries to analyze and control what is happening in the present, and dreams and wonders about the future. His thoughts, however, are often colored by his tendency to fantasize, as on the evening he spends with Mattie, he almost believes the two of them are married until they are startled by the cat jumping off the rocker. Ethan's interior life wavers between self-confidence and self-deprecation, and as we will see, he has the ability of expanding realities or illusions to either enhance or belittle himself.

What sets Ethan's mind to work now is the sight of Denis Eady dancing with Mattie Silver; Ethan is jealous of young Eady's dashing ways, so to bolster his own ego, he recalls some of the things which have made Mattie precious to him. Mrs. Wharton's purpose is to introduce us to Mattie and to prepare us with suggestions and hints for the dramatic appearance of Zeena. Mattie is first identified as Zeena's cousin, come to Starkfield as a household helper, and allowed to go into town from the farm when there are festivities.

Ethan has liked Mattie since the first day when he met her at the train and found her the happy opposite of cold and complaining Zeena. In contrast to Zeena, as well, Mattie has a sensitive nature, and she is able to communicate with Ethan and Ethan with her. There is none of the terrible silence and isolation that dominates Ethan's marriage to Zeena. Ethan is particularly pleased that Mattie shares his appreciation of natural beauty, and of "meanings" behind natural phenomena, such as granite outcroppings caused by an ice age.

This kind of communication between Ethan and Mattie is based on their mutual, unvoiced and unanalyzed awe and appreciation of nature. Mattie's perception of a particularly beautiful vista as though it were a painting is the best case in point. Ethan regards the statement as the paradigm case of definition of natural beauty, and he feels his "secret soul" stirred because he has shared a feeling with her that he never could have with Zeena. We should pay close attention to the words Mrs. Wharton uses to describe Ethan's thoughts. Especially when he thinks of Mattie, Ethan tries to escape the reality of his marriage by indulging in self-illusion.

While he stands outside the window, Ethan's thoughts have run through a cheering sequence of memories of himself and Mattie. Now Mrs. Wharton further prepares us for the action and complications of the novel by having Ethan remember his fear that Mattie has no real affection for him and that Zeena will find out his growing love for Mattie. This train of thought is triggered by the sight of Mattie treating Denis Eady to some of the mannerisms and affectations which Ethan thought she reserved for him alone. The "latent fears" which he forces on himself are as important a part of his psyche as his tendency to use self-illusion as an escape. Ethan's fears cause as much confused thinking as do his dreams. Some of his fears are founded in reality and reflect Zeena's disapproval of his favoring of Mattie, while others are just as illusory as his dreams.

In reading through Ethan's catalogue of fears we have the opportunity of learning more about Zeena: while she is "sickly," Ethan is suspicious of how sick she really is — he correctly suspects that she may be feigning part of her illness. Ethan's memory of the morning when Zeena had observed him shaving serves to foreshadow her character and physical appearance before her dramatic appearance on the Frome back porch: she has a gray complexion, high cheek bones, and a drawling voice which can dominate Ethan by whining plaintively or by showing sudden obstinance. Zeena's vindictive nature casts a pall of dominance over Ethan and Mattie throughout the book and is one of the causes of their attempted suicide.

Ethan's remembrance of his fears concludes his retrospective thinking at the window and coincides with the breaking-up of the dance inside the church. Made shy both by Mattie's attentions to Denis Eady and by his own recollections of Zeena,

Ethan decides to test Mattie and see if she will accompany Eady. Mattie refuses Eady and as she goes off alone to walk home, Ethan catches up with her, now made happy by her "choice" of him over Eady. He feels that his masculinity is assured—the fear that Mattie really likes Denis Eady is temporarily quashed, and because he believes he has done something "arch and ingenious," his sense of masculine mastery of the entire situation is enhanced.

Mrs. Wharton, however, undercuts Ethan's sense of superiority with one skillful stroke: Ethan comes forth with the ineffective pronouncement, "Come along." Ethan uses the same phrase again on their walk home as a substitute for eloquence. Mrs. Wharton makes apparent the difficulty Ethan has in communicating even with Mattie. His romantic dreams go far beyond his willingness to express his affection in words or action: he has only begun to break through the barriers of silence and isolation which have grown up as a result of the lack of communication in his marriage.

Stopping for a moment above the Corbury hill, Mattie tells Ethan about Ned Hale and Ruth Varnum's brush with death that evening when their sled narrowly missed hitting an elm tree on its downhill run. This other couple serves as a sort of symbol for Ethan and Mattie of the happiness that they might have, and Ethan in particular bases some of his illusions about himself and Mattie on Ned and Ruth's actions. Ethan uses this opportunity to brag about his prowess as a sled steersman and to promise to bring Mattie the next evening if there is a moon. The description of Ned and Ruth's near-accident on Corbury hill plus an earlier mention of the coasting-ground foreshadow the sledding mishap, providing an atmosphere of increasing inevitability as the hints of the crash accumulate.

When Mattie suddenly flounces away from Ethan, he decides that she indeed does not care for him, and once more his attitude sinks from joyful confidence to despair. Mrs. Wharton makes it quite evident that Ethan's incapability of declaring his love to Mattie makes him "attach a fantastic importance to every change in her look and tone." Ethan's romantic illusions are caused largely by fancied indications of approval or disapproval from Mattie. Insecure about his status with Mattie, Ethan intimates that she rejects him because she will be leaving the Fromes to marry Denis Eady.

Mattie, however, interprets Ethan to mean that Zeena wants her gone. She apologizes for her inadequacies as a houseworker, then asks Ethan to clarify what he means. Ethan, reassured that Mattie is not about to marry, limits himself to the once again anticlimactic "Come along." Having produced a situation of anxiety for Mattie, he is unable to immediately resolve it because he cannot bring himself to say what lies behind his concern for her welfare.

Approaching the farmhouse, Ethan once more satisfies himself that Mattie wants to stay with the Fromes, and draws her to him, again reassured that she will not marry Denis Eady. Physical contact here substitutes for communication. As Ethan and Mattie pass the Frome family graveyard, Ethan is reminded that he used to regard it as an omen that he would never find release and freedom from the life he was confined to with Zeena. Now, momentarily satisfied of the stability of his life with Mattie at the farmhouse, Ethan thinks of his forebears as "lovers once" who will help him win Mattie. When she stumbles and holds on to Ethan to keep her balance, Ethan uses the opportunity to put his arm around Mattie, thereby confirming for himself his role as protector, and affirming his "vision" of a life together with her.

Throughout the walk home from the dance, Ethan has abandoned himself to his romantic feelings and his attraction to Mattie. His perception of what actually happens is distorted and colored by his need to create reassuring illusions. He makes almost no attempt to really communicate with Mattie; instead, he drifts into fantasy.

Ethan's love for Mattie as yet remains one-sided and is fed on illusion because it is hard for him to draw away from the patterns of silence and isolation in his life. He still cannot be

sure that Mattie feels any true affection for him, even though his
groping attempts at communication on the walk home have
confirmed for him that Mattie does not want to leave the Frome
farm. The closest he can come to telling Mattie how he feels is
to pull her to him and whisper that they will always be together.
Ironically, they are passing the graveyard as he pronounces these
words, and the death in life after the catastrophe is here
foreshadowed.

With the graveyard on his mind, the sight of a dead
cucumber vine reminds Ethan of a funeral crape, and he half
wishes it were there for Zeena; Ethan's feeling of happiness with
Mattie has been thwarted by the thought of Zeena, and Ethan
subconsciously wishes she were dead. Other evidences of this
wish occur when Ethan and Mattie cannot find the back-door
key and Ethan fleetingly thinks that tramps might have broken
into the house.

The appearance of Zeena which now occurs has been carefully prepared by Mrs. Wharton. Zeena's "sickness" and dis-
agreeable nature have been hinted about, and various of her
unattractive physical characteristics have been described. When
she opens the door it seems to Ethan that he has never seen his
wife so completely before. Coming after his illusions about
future happiness with Mattie, the sight of Zeena has almost the
significance of an epiphany for Ethan. Mrs. Wharton's description of Zeena carefully emphasizes the hard and cold nature of
the woman, "tall and angular," with a "flat breast," "puckered
throat," and "projecting wrist." She is the ugly reality from
which Ethan tries to escape in his dreams of Mattie.

Zeena has felt "so mean" she could not sleep. In colloquial
usage the words denote that she has felt ill, but there is clearly
an ironic connotation of Zeena's vindictiveness intended as
well. After scolding Ethan and Mattie about the snow on their
shoes, Zeena starts to go off to bed; Ethan does not want to follow
her up but he thinks he sees Mattie blink him a warning, so he
gives in to his wife.

It is almost as if Zeena wields some kind of power over Ethan. He cannot really communicate with her, and over the course of their marriage he has become acquiescent and obeisant around Zeena. Only when Zeena is not present the following night is there any domestic peace for Ethan, and the short experience which he does have is the basis of his decision that he should make known to Mattie his love for her.

Ethan and Mattie's domestic idyll is made possible by Zeena's overnight trip to Bettsbridge to see Dr. Buck. Waking early, however, Ethan does not find out about Zeena's plans until after he has worked part of the morning outside. It is fresh and clear and Ethan is full of thoughts about Mattie. Chiding himself for not having kissed her, he marvels that before the events of last night he would hardly have dared entertain such a notion. The walk home served to assimilate many of the feelings which he has had about Mattie; a sort of climax in the story has been reached: Ethan has now definitely decided that he could be happy with her and he needs only the proof that happiness could be attained. Zeena's absence gives Ethan and Mattie a chance to further break down the barriers which prevent them from true communication.

In preparation for the evening idyll, Mrs. Wharton has Ethan recall Mattie's background and the details of how she came to live with the Fromes. If Mattie's accomplishments such as making candy and trimming hats seem frivolous in the face of the hard work she is required to do for Zeena, these abilities represent a youthful and happy personality which is able to entertain itself with frivolity instead of moping in self-pity about negligible or imagined ills as Zeena does.

Mattie is in most ways the opposite of Zeena; Mattie is young, happy, healthy, and pretty while Zeena is unhappy, ugly, sickly, and seven years older than Ethan. Mrs. Wharton works to make Mattie naturally appealing while she presents Zeena as an unlikable and cold woman. These portraits in the body of the novel make the epilogue all the more ironic; while Zeena undergoes no really remarkable change, she does shoulder the responsibility of caring for the two cripples and in particular of enduring the whining and petulant Mattie.

At this state in the book, however, it is Zeena who is whining and petulant and Zeena's presence which must be endured. Ethan's fear that Zeena may discover his affection for Mattie is so great that as he is about to leave for town with a load of lumber, he changes his mind and decides to return to the house before making the delivery. It is fortunate that he does so, because he discovers Zeena's decision to make a trip to Bettsbridge to consult Dr. Buck, who has never treated her before.

Ethan's first thought is that such trips have cost him a good deal of money in patent remedies which have no effect on Zeena's sicknesses; he disregards these unpleasant recollections when it occurs to him that Zeena's absence will give him and Mattie a night alone together. In addition, his fears that Zeena may suspect his love for Mattie are allayed because it is confirmed that she was indeed feeling ill the previous night. Just as he had told an untruth the night before to avoid going upstairs with Zeena, Ethan now invents a reason that he cannot drive Zeena to the train.

This time, however, Ethan's alibi of going into town to be paid for the lumber is more acceptable to Zeena, and Ethan realizes that it was not a good idea to let Zeena know that he had any money before she went on one of her expensive journeys to doctors. Such considerations are quickly put aside, however, as Ethan contemplates the evening with Mattie. The falsehood he has told will come back to haunt him because Zeena later justifies her hiring of a girl to replace Mattie on the basis of the fifty-dollar advance Ethan mentioned.

After Zeena has left with Jotham Powell, Ethan goes off to town to deliver the lumber to Andrew Hale. Although his affection for Mattie is increasing, he has not had sufficient impetus to tell her. His goal is to enjoy an evening with Mattie and without Zeena; on the way to town his mind is busy conjuring up pictures of what the evening will be like. It is important to note that

Ethan visualizes nothing illicit or immoral; all he hopes for is an evening of laughing and talking before the fire. Such thoughts bring Ethan to remember his college days and awake in him the deadened social sense. Laughing and talking also reminds Ethan of the silence of one sort or another he has known since his days at college.

The theme of silence, adumbrated before this point, now explicitly appears and is discussed with reference to Ethan's past. We recall that some of the symptoms of the silence surrounding Ethan were his inability to communicate with Zeena and his halting efforts to say something significant to Mattie. The silence imposed by his marriage to Zeena is one of the causes of Ethan's need for illusion. Illusion in turn reinforces the silence by helping Ethan to avoid communication by fantasizing. The background of Ethan's marriage to Zeena is here revealed so that the evening with Mattie in which silence is partially conquered will be prepared for. We find out in greater depth the isolation of Ethan's mind in a silent house with a silent woman.

Before her death Ethan's mother had become more and more silent as the winter drew on, claiming that she did not talk because she was listening to the wind outside the house. The silence his mother imposed enforced a terrible loneliness on Ethan which was broken only when Zeena arrived to help with the nursing. Talkative and efficient, her presence filled an immense chasm for Ethan, and after his mother's death he could not bear to have her leave because he dreaded being alone.

Significantly, Ethan now thinks that he might not have married Zeena if it had been spring instead of winter when his mother passed away. He realizes that his fear of loneliness rather than love for Zeena prompted their marriage. When Ethan wanted to move away from Starkfield, Zeena resisted, beginning to widen the control over Ethan she had assumed when she took over the task of nursing his mother. Then Zeena became both sickly and silent, and she enforced the silence of her life on Ethan until the arrival of Mattie brought him some possibility of communication.

Now we discover another reason why Ethan is relieved by Zeena's trip to Bettsbridge: he has thought at various times that Zeena's silence concealed mysterious, almost sinister, powers of observation and intuition; now he is sure that she was in reality ill the night before, and that all he has to worry about is how much of his money she will spend on the trip.

When Ethan asks Andrew Hale for payment in advance of the time he usually gets his money, he is refused. Hale is building a house for the soon to be married Ned and Ruth, and is generally short of money anyhow. The mention of the impending marriage causes Ethan to recall that the seven years of his marriage to Zeena seem but a short time to Andrew Hale. Later, the sight of Ned and Ruth kissing amidst the Varnum spruces makes Ethan sad because he had had to hide his love for Mattie when they stood on that spot the night before.

Driving home, Ethan passes the family cemetery again, where the tombstone of Ethan and Endurance Frome proclaims that they shared fifty years of wedded bliss. The epitaph seems ironic to Ethan. Recently reminded of seven years' endurance of Zeena, he wonders if people might someday say that about the two of them. More important as a parallel to the previous night's action, Ethan's thoughts show that he now seriously does consider himself immutably married to Zeena, and that he briefly realizes his thoughts of being buried in the cemetery with Mattie were fantasy. The headstone is doubly ironic as well because, in the end, it is Zeena who must forego her hypochondriac indulgence and prove herself in the role of "endurance" in anything but peaceful circumstances as she ministers for years to the two crippled victims of the sledding crash.

The events of the night before are carefully paralleled in order to draw attention in a dramatic and climactic moment to the difference between Zeena and Mattie. When Mattie lets Ethan in the locked back door, striking the same pose that Zeena did the night before, Ethan is struck by the immense difference between the young, warm, and feminine Mattie and his old, cold, and hard Zeena.

Mrs. Wharton carefully structures the events in this way to allow Mattie to demonstrate her feelings for Ethan without oral communication. Neither of the two lovers is ready to make a direct declaration, but now Mattie has her chance to show that Ethan is someone special to her by breaking the coldness of the house and of his marriage and by bringing him a sense of domestic happiness. Mattie simply adds a red ribbon to her hairdo, acts cheerfully, laughs, and prepares Ethan's favorite dishes for supper. Indeed, the house has been transformed into a place of warmth and love, and Ethan's earlier thoughts that Mattie could be a good housekeeper if she had someone to care for her seem to be confirmed.

Both Mattie and Ethan are inhibited during the meal by the mention of Zeena's name, and the power of her "presence" experienced on the walk the night before, begins to assert itself. The cat was introduced at the beginning of chapter four and its importance as a surrogate for Zeena slowly emerges. First, Mattie nearly trips over the cat, then the cat sits in Zeena's chair during the meal, and finally, it causes the pickle dish to be broken. The cat continues to represent Zeena later in the evening when Ethan and Mattie sit next to the fire, but its major role is breaking the pickle dish.

The breaking of the dish is a climactic event in the story. It is a simple item of glassware, perhaps, but it is appropriate to the mood of the evening; its purpose is to hold pickles, one of Ethan's favorite foods. Its color is red, and red fits in with the festive red ribbon that Mattie wears in her hair. But the pickle dish was a wedding present to Zeena, and it is one of her most precious things, kept on the top shelf of the china closet.

Having used the pickle dish in the first place is a trespass against Zeena; now having it broken would call for an explanation which neither Ethan nor Mattie is prepared to give. Therefore, Ethan is seized with the "latent resolution" which he has kept submerged under Zeena's domination. Clearly, unless he manages the situation, he will fail to honor the love he feels for Mattie. To protect her from Zeena's wrath over the broken pickle dish is a proof of both his manhood and his love.

Of course, it is ironic that a broken pickle dish is at the root of the sudden emergence of Ethan's assertiveness, and it may even evoke laughter to realize that Ethan has known the same feeling of power only when moving logs downhill to his sawmill. But in another way, it is quite a considerable thing that Ethan does. Earlier, when Ethan was talking with Andrew Hale, we found that he had no ability to lie, and he was unable to claim the money that was rightly his, even though not customarily paid at that time. Now Ethan deliberately conceives of an act of deceit to cover up for Mattie, and in so doing he feels a sense of masculine dominance he has never known with Zeena.

After dinner, the crisis of the pickle dish is temporarily forgotten, and Ethan and Mattie experience the kind of domestic bliss that they might have without Zeena. Although they are temporarily reminded of Zeena when Mattie sits in her mistress' chair, and this makes them uneasy, they nevertheless overcome the silence and experience for a short time the sensation of a stable relationship. Their conversation is about the most common and normal of things, but it establishes a communication and a conviviality which Ethan has never experienced with Zeena.

Ethan feels happy, fulfilled, and masculine. As he had the night before, he lets his imagination go and allows himself to glory in the thought that this is his normal way of life, and that he does have a beautiful and healthy wife in Mattie. He can talk of going coasting with her as if they have the choice of doing it any night they wish. He enjoys the sense of masculine superiority by trying to make Mattie admit she would be afraid. The reference to coasting is, of course, another portent of the fate of the two.

Eased by the comfortable atmosphere which has been built up, Ethan tells Mattie that he saw Ned and Ruth kissing that afternoon; he has thought that such an opening might lead to a caress or even a kiss from Mattie, but he finds that he cannot carry thought into action—he feels constrained when Mattie blushes. Just before the suicide attempt, Mattie and Ethan actually do kiss at the spot, somehow identifying their love with the open and approved love of Ned and Ruth.

To keep the conversation going, Ethan brings up the subject of marriage, first in relation to Ned and Ruth, and then with regard to Mattie. Her reaction is that Ethan knows Zeena to be dissatisfied with her, and that Zeena's peculiar behavior the night before had something to do with it. This is the first time that the two of them have spoken so openly of Zeena, and they agree that she is unpredictable. Their conversation is a foreshadowing of Zeena's decision to fire Mattie and get a new houseworker. Ethan reacts by putting the matter out of mind; it is typical of him to behave in this way. He wants to savor as much of the evening as possible without any thought of Zeena intruding into his dreams of bliss with Mattie. As well, we have seen how he has been dominated by Zeena as long as they have been married.

Mrs. Wharton's characterization of Ethan is such that he is not the kind of man who might meet the problem head on, declare his love to Mattie, and find some way of leaving Zeena for a new life. Ethan must be forced by circumstances; where another man might see what loving Mattie implies, Ethan does not plan ahead or speculate on the various courses of action that are available, and this characteristic, related to his tendency to escape reality through self-illusion, is a partial cause of the tragedy.

Holding on to a piece of the material that Mattie is sewing, Ethan feels very close to her, and from the expression on her face he thinks she understands the feeling also. They sit entranced until the cat startles them by jumping out of Zeena's rocking chair and setting it to rocking. Once again they are reminded of Zeena by the cat and the mood is broken entirely. Ethan is suddenly conscious of how much of a dream the evening has been; the reality which they have avoided makes him feel weary and defeated. Mattie is also tired, and as she begins to roll up her sewing Ethan kisses the material as a last gesture of the intimacy of their evening.

After doing their chores they go off to bed; once he is alone Ethan realizes that there has been no physical contact since he touched Mattie's hand at the dinner table. But it is not physical contact which is important. Both Ethan and Mattie have reached a point where they realize that they have a definite affection for each other. A kind of communication has been achieved which was only hinted at during the walk the night before and on previous occasions such as the summer picnic at Shadow Pond. There now exists a very real basis in shared experience for Mattie and Ethan to believe that they can be happy together and that they are indeed in love.

## IMAGERY, SYMBOLISM, STYLE

The symbolic setting in winter and in Starkfield continues to dominate the imagery and symbolism as they do throughout the novel. Note that Mrs. Wharton generally uses imagery appropriate to the setting of the novel and to experiences her characters might have had. She does not inject inappropriate comparisons or ideas into the novel. Imagery associated with winter typically characterizes Zeena, while Mattie is often represented by imagery of spring and summer. Ethan is naturally attracted to the imagery of warmth and life surrounding Mattie. Associated with these winter/summer patterns of imagery and symbol are the motifs of (1) sickness, death, and the graveyard, and (2) silence and isolation.

At the beginning of part one Mrs. Wharton sets the scene for Ethan Frome's tragedy: the three and a half days in time which the story covers are at the height of winter and as the story opens the first paragraph describes the winter night. It is windy, and there are two feet of snow on the ground; the stars shine like icicles and Orion seems to be a "cold fire." The bringing together of two opposite terms like this is an oxymoron and it serves to emphasize in a particular way the nature of the thing described. Here, of course, the object is a star, but Mrs. Wharton has it set in a "sky of iron" and the total effect of the description is to give us a feeling of the bitterness and hardness of the winter.

The description is appropriate to the symbolic role the winter plays in the book and is a most effective way to introduce Ethan's walk into town. We note that on the walk home when Mattie assures Ethan she does not want to leave the Frome household, "the iron heavens seemed to melt and rain down sweetness."

We see, then that the antithesis to symbolic cold is the warmth that Ethan finds in his own thoughts and even more in Mattie Silver. On his way to the church Ethan finds the cloudy "meanings" in his thoughts set up a glow in his brain. When he reaches the church, he decides to stay in "pure and frosty darkness," analogous to the silence and isolation he experiences and in opposition to the happy sociability of the interior of the church (which he sees as in "a mist of heat" caused by the "volcanic fires" from the stove in the room).

Indeed, Ethan feels that Mattie's effect on him is like "the lighting of a fire on a cold hearth." Her face seems to him "like a window that has caught the sunset." On the way home from the dance, when Ethan reveals to Mattie that he had been hiding while she talked to Denis Eady, "her wonder and his laughter ran together like spring rills in a thaw." Mattie's changes in mood seem to Ethan to be like "the flit of a bird in the branches." When Ethan has finally gotten up the courage to put his arm around Mattie, he feels that walking with her is like "floating on a summer stream."

In stark contrast to these few citations of warm natural imagery are those which represent the cold, the isolation, and the death of spirit inherent in the winter and particularly in the Frome farmhouse. On their walk home Ethan and Mattie see farmhouses which all seem to them "mute and cold as a gravestone." At the Frome farmhouse they see the dead cucumber vine "like the crape streamer tied to the door for a death." And once they are inside the kitchen, it has "the deadly chill of a vault after the dry cold of the night." These images are related to the fascination which Ethan finds in his family graveyard, and they are also appropriate to the living death that Ethan and

Mattie experience for the years after their accident. Their lives do indeed become cold and dead, and Ethan will find himself even more silent and isolated than before Mattie came into his life.

The bleak and cold imagery is directly related to Zeena when Ethan sees her before her trip to Bettsbridge and she sits in "the pale light reflected from the banks of snow," which makes "her face look more than usually drawn and bloodless," and makes her other unattractive features more apparent. Immediately after Zeena leaves with Jotham Powell, however, the kitchen seems more comfortable and inviting because Mattie and Ethan are alone, although Ethan stays for only a short time.

Once again during the evening that Ethan and Mattie spend in each other's company we see how Mrs. Wharton uses the imagery of warmth and cold to complement characterization. The imagery associated with Mattie is now that of summer and natural life: her face seems "like a wheat field under a summer breeze"; her pronunciation of the word "married" seems to invoke "a rustling covert leading to enchanted glades"; and the action of her hands over her sewing resembles birds building their nests.

Mrs. Wharton's descriptive imagery is one of the most important features of her simple and efficient prose style. We notice that descriptions are not lavished through the novel to provide background color; when they occur they serve a definite stylistic and structural purpose. The imagery cited above in relation to the characters is practically all of the imagery in the first part of the novel. There is not very much of it, and it is not ostentatiously woven into long passages of description. It is simply and sometimes subtly stated and it is always appropriate to the characterizations which Mrs. Wharton is building. In addition, it fits into the symbolic and thematic levels of the novel to provide an economy of construction and of meaning that may seem too simple to pay attention to before the strength and genius of Mrs. Wharton's style is apprehended.

The ease with which the book can be read may be deceptive: Mrs. Wharton has orchestrated all the levels of meaning in her writing so well that it may take a second reading to appreciate just how skillfully it is done and how appropriate it is to the novel. As much as the tragedy of Ethan Frome takes place in a stark moral and physical environment, the prose which describes it is similarly stark and barren.

## PART II: CHAPTERS 6-9

### ACTION, CHARACTERIZATION, THEME

The action of part one has established the basis for the events moving to the tragedy in part two. Part two consists of chapters six through nine and in time elapsed it covers about two days, from the morning after Ethan and Mattie's blissful evening to the smashup itself. Part two concludes the "vision" of the narrator of the frame story and is followed by the epilogue which gives us a full realization of the extent of the tragedy drawn out over twenty years.

Ethan's happiness is a product of his own self-deception. He still has not considered carefully the implications of his love for Mattie nor has he really tried to project what Zeena's reaction would be, other than that she would not like it. One of Ethan's most important decisions later in the novel revolves about his thoughts of whether or not he could leave Zeena. For now however, all he can remember is the "vision" of the previous evening. He thinks of it in his customary dreamy manner, but as he has done in the past, he still cannot bring himself to openly declare his feelings.

When Jotham Powell has left the room and Ethan is alone with Mattie, he wants to make a romantic speech about this being their last chance to be alone together. But his resolve fails him as it did when he tried to speak to Mattie on the walk home and could only say "come along." Here he can only bring himself to tell Mattie that he will be home for dinner. Only when the crisis of Mattie's impending dismissal is at hand does Ethan muster the fortitude to speak outright, and even then he is limited because of his indecision about how to handle Zeena and the effect of her domination over him.

Ethan's immediate concern is to get glue to fix the broken pickle dish, and this he tries to do in town after he has delivered more lumber to Andrew Hale. But all nature conspires against him. One of his horses slips and cuts a leg on the ice and then the sleety rain makes the loading of the cart take an extra long time. Note that here Mrs. Wharton's memory for detail fails her, and she transforms lumber into "tree trunks." Earlier, on Ethan's first trip into town, she did the same thing, changing the lumber loaded at the sawmill into "logs" unloaded at Andrew Hale's. Despite such small inconsistencies, her purpose is to delay Ethan; he has to stay at the farm until after dinner, and he is frustrated from talking with Mattie again because Jotham Powell is present for the meal. Despite his haste once in town, Ethan is frustrated in his effort to buy glue at the Eady's store and must go to the widow Homan's before he finds it.

When Ethan finally reaches home, he is too late; Zeena has arrived, but has said nothing and gone to her room. Ethan now thinks that he will fix the broken dish at night; but Zeena's return makes him worried and he asks Jotham Powell to stay for supper as a restraining influence. Jotham's refusal seems to him an ominous hint of Zeena's vindictive mood. Yet when he returns to the house, Mattie's preparations for supper make it seem as warm and hospitable as the evening before.

Mrs. Wharton's fine sense of dramatic irony operates here to set the stage with the momentary recollection of the happiness of the last evening as a prelude to the anxiety and grief which is to come. Zeena's announcement that Mattie must go will kill the false sense of security that Ethan has harbored and break the illusion that he and Mattie will be able to endure Zeena together.

The confrontation occurs in the bedroom of the Frome house. Remembering Ethan's flashbacks, we should associate the room with Zeena, and if her cold presence rules the house it is especially prevalent in this room. Here she has nursed her sicknesses, and here she has asserted herself over Ethan with her malicious sense of observation, as when she chided him about starting to shave every morning after Mattie had come to live at the Fromes. Note that Ethan thinks best outside this room, as he did on the morning after he walked Mattie home, and as he will do on the night to come, staying out of the bedroom and sleeping fitfully in his "study."

We find that the confrontation of Ethan and Zeena follows a familiar pattern; the same sort of thing happens each time Zeena returns from one of her expeditions to doctors in other towns. This time we see in detail the way in which Zeena is able to assert her dominance over Ethan. She first announces that she is the victim of "complications" but she maintains a cunning attitude of ascendancy. She is successful; despite his knowledge that Zeena plays upon her sickliness to her own advantage, Ethan is swayed by her story and feels compassion for her because he really does believe that she may have a serious illness.

Zeena is quick to sense her advantage and she changes her tone to one of resolution when she informs Ethan that Dr. Buck has prescribed that she do no more work around the house. With the help of a relative, she has hired a new girl to come and assume the household duties. Ethan is so thunderstruck by the potential blow to his pocketbook that he does not think of the implications for Mattie. His anger is roused but in the argument which follows he is forced to admit lamely that he was unable to get the money from Andrew Hale and he feels his position weakened at almost being caught in a lie.

But Zeena has saved her trump card, and Ethan thinks that the scene is over before she plays it. Her skillful ability to catch Ethan off guard provides her with great amusement. When Ethan is startled at hearing Zeena say that the cost of Mattie's keep will be saved, she laughs, and it is the first time in their seven-year marriage that Ethan can recall her having laughed. Then, Mrs. Wharton injects another touch of irony into the scene by having Mattie cheerfully call the two to supper just after Zeena has scornfully referred to the girl as a "pauper."

Again, Ethan is faced with the comparison between the two women which he cannot help but draw. Zeena has conquered him and he knows it; but Ethan tries once more to change Zeena's mind by exhorting her with a defense of Mattie's work. Her calm, inexorable authority prevails over Ethan's momentary wrath, however, and Ethan is struck even more by the sense of his weakness and powerlessness. As Zeena goes on to tell him that the new girl will arrive the following day and that therefore Mattie will have to leave, Ethan is finally gripped by the understanding of just how well Zeena controls him and rules the house.

All the forebodings of Zeena's power have finally been proven true. She seems now to Ethan to be an "alien presence," an "evil energy" which has finally struck out at him from behind a front of brooding observation. For an instant his realization that Zeena knows very well how much Mattie means brings him to the point of striking her. But no sooner has he conceived the idea than he abandons it: her power is in fact complete. He retreats from the bedroom.

Ethan finds Mattie downstairs in the kitchen, the part of the house that she had made a happy place for him the night before. As Ethan confronts her, there are reminiscences of the night before in her warm demeanor. But his argument with Zeena has pushed him beyond the feeling of domestic bliss which prevailed in relation to Mattie: without explaining why Ethan embraces and kisses Mattie, caught up in love for her and revulsion against Zeena.

One of the best indications of Ethan's pent-up romantic illusions is the way that he breaks the news to Mattie. Instead of explaining the sequence of events which has led to his anxiety, it is "as if he saw her drowning in a dream," when he tells her he will never let her go. Then, ashamed of his inconsiderate outburst, Ethan explains to Mattie the circumstances of Zeena's decision to dismiss her. Finally, moved by his anticipation of what her plight will be when thrown on the mercies of the outside world, Ethan is moved to swear that he will reverse Zeena's decision.

Mrs. Wharton here dramatically and superbly undercuts Ethan's attempt at a manly defense of Mattie by simply describing Zeena's entrance into the kitchen. Ethan's words are stilled in mid-sentence as he hears his wife behind him. We are left to imagine Ethan's silent frustration as Mrs. Wharton tells us what Zeena says and does at the table. It is indeed almost as if she is an alien presence in regard to Ethan: her dominance is such that it can strike him dumb after the greatest demonstration he has ever made of his love for Mattie.

Triumphant after her quarrel with Ethan, Zeena enjoys her victory by flaunting her power over the two lesser beings of her household. Zeena has the absolute power of a queen and her smiles at the supper table only enforce further the fact of her rule. When Zeena has left the room to get her stomach powders, the semblance of the momentary peace in the kitchen to the night before is an ironic calm before the storm.

Zeena's impressive and stony self-control is broken when she finds the carefully arranged pieces of the shattered pickle dish. She is visibly angered, and has even shed two tears; but when Ethan makes his feeble attempt at lying to protect Mattie, Zeena's self-control returns and she laughs again with the delight of having caught Ethan in a lie. Mattie confesses and is scolded severely by Zeena. Ethan's helplessness is evident not from any description of his actions, but, as before, from the sheer absence of any mention of him. Zeena holds complete power over him and, his attempt at lying found out, he will not challenge her even to protect Mattie. The force of Zeena's anger about the pickle dish is such that it brings her to sobbing for a moment before she regains her hard composure and leaves the room.

After the storm and bombast of the argument between Zeena and Ethan and of Zeena's scolding of Mattie, there follows a period of agonized and quiet thinking for Ethan. When he is sure that his wife is asleep Ethan goes downstairs to his cold "study" to mull over the meanings of what has happened that night. He takes with him the note that Mattie had left him earlier in the evening. It is the first thing she has ever written him, and in a way, it is the first real sign of communication of her affection for him.

Ethan is moved to thoughts of revolt against Zeena's rule; the defeat he suffered at her hands has nettled him. He remembers the story of a man who lived nearby who escaped from a tyrannous wife by fleeing to the West with his lover and leaving his farm to his wife. Ethan thinks the plan is a good one and begins to write the letter to Zeena which Mattie later finds, but once again money is a problem; he hasn't enough even to pay for his train fare, let alone provide some to leave for Zeena.

Although we might be able to think of ways for Ethan to escape, he cannot; he finds himself a prisoner of circumstance: there is no way for him to flee with Mattie now that he really wants to. Lying down to cry over his fate, he sees the beauty of the night landscape before he drops off to sleep. Again the coasting accident is foreshadowed as Ethan fleetingly remembers that this is the night of the full moon when he had promised to take Mattie coasting.

After Mattie has come and found him and they have begun the morning chores, things do not seem so bleak to Ethan. His self-deceptive optimism about Mattie takes over his thoughts, and despite his earlier realization that Zeena's decision is unchangeable, he decides that things are not hopeless and that he will keep Mattie at home.

Jotham Powell, however, knows the strength of Zeena's decision and stoically accepts it, although he does not contradict Ethan's reservations about Mattie's departure. When the two men go inside for breakfast, Zeena confirms to Jotham that Daniel Byrne is coming to pick up Mattie's trunk that afternoon. As he was the night before, Ethan is again a silent subject of his despot.

Mrs. Wharton uses the same technique she has used earlier in the novel to present Ethan's subservience—not a mention of his thoughts or intentions is made, although we know that he is present and that he had intended to use this opportunity to protest Mattie's dismissal. Jotham's comment at the end of the scene is the ironic climax to another of Ethan's failures to assert himself over his wife.

Ethan's reaction to defeat is one of rebellion; humiliated in front of Mattie, he starts off to Starkfield afoot, determined to do something to change the situation. The springlike morning reminds him of Mattie and provides him with even more incentive. Ethan decides to try Andrew Hale once again for the money he is owed; meeting Mrs. Hale and her son driving a sled down the road, however, Ethan stops them. He says practically nothing while Mrs. Hale prattles about her husband's lumbago and about their sympathy for Zeena's new illness and for Ethan's ability to endure all of his ill fortune.

After Mrs. Hale has driven off, Ethan thinks for a moment that because the Hales are sympathetic they will surely advance him his money. But then he catches himself up short with the realization that he cannot deceive two kindly people into lending him money that they need. Ethan now decides that he must accept the sad reality of his lot.

While a modern reader might feel that Ethan is ineffectual for not aggressively demanding from Andrew Hale what is rightfully owed to him, this would be a misunderstanding of Mrs. Wharton's purpose. She wants to make abundantly clear that Ethan is inescapably bound within the little segment of society that he inhabits. Part of his tragedy is that having aspirations and dreams which would take him beyond the icy world of Starkfield, his fate is to serve out his life chained to a frigid, quarrelsome wife and to the crippled remains of a beautiful girl. There can be no possible alternative of escape in Ethan's mind when he is faced with the decision of whether or not to try to commit suicide with Mattie. Turned away from the Hales by his own conscience, Ethan walks back to the farm to see Mattie leave.

Once home, Ethan is furious to find that Zeena has told Mattie she must bring down her trunk alone because Daniel Byrne must tend to his horse. Zeena — the supreme ruler of her domain — sits by the fire reading a book on kidney aliments. Going to help Mattie, Ethan sees that her room has been stripped bare of the personal possessions and decorations which had made it uniquely hers. Ethan comforts the crying girl, who had been told she would not see him again. If ever we might expect Ethan to assert himself against Zeena, it is now. But when she calls upstairs for them to hurry, Ethan cannot bring himself to challenge her rule.

Ethan takes the trunk outside to Daniel Byrne, and then with a supreme effort of will, he decides to face up to Zeena and defy her wish that Jotham drive Mattie to the station. The confrontation occurs after lunch: Ethan refuses to allow Jotham to be the driver, and he dismisses Zeena's wish that he stay home to fix the stove for the new girl. But he cannot completely defy Zeena because he makes the excuse that he has something to attend to in the town as the reason that he will accompany Mattie.

Gripped with the force of his anger as he harnesses the sorrel for the trip, Ethan recalls the similar springish day a little more than a year before when he had gone to pick up Mattie at the station. His reminiscences are not detailed, but they prepare us for the mood of sad remembrance which will preface the decision of the lovers to die together. Mattie waits for him in his study, the only part of the house which she can identify with Ethan, and he is overcome on finding her with the sense of the unreality of her departure. He does not know that she has found his letter to Zeena.

Mrs. Wharton gives us three indications of the relation between Ethan and Mattie as another prelude to the revelation which is about to occur: on the drive to the train Ethan and Mattie will discover for the first time how much they love each other and why they would prefer to die together rather than live apart. In order not to break the mood which she is building, Mrs. Wharton does not again bring Zeena into the action. Satisfied with the victory of her eviction, Zeena has retired to her bedroom without a word of goodbye to Mattie.

Ethan feels almost happy at the beginning of the ride; the sense of unreality which he feels is appropriate to this journey because it will be a trip of discovery and happiness until the force of time and circumstance brings the lovers to their attempt at death. When Ethan does not turn onto the shortest route to the station, Mattie immediately senses where he is going. Shadow Pond had been the site of the church picnic the previous summer where Mattie's feelings for Ethan had first coalesced into love.

The name "Shadow" is suggestive of the memories that both lovers have of the spot; as well, it connotes the inability that Mattie and Ethan have of really communicating their feelings to each other. The incident in which Ethan found her locket is symbolic of the love that he found with it. It is not unreasonable to suppose that the gold trinket represents Mattie's heart. But, at the time it happened, the incident was only a portent of what might come to pass. Similarly, this return visit to the spot is inarticulate; it causes Ethan and Mattie to ponder their love without speaking out about it; it is Mattie who realizes that they must give in to the pressures of time and continue on their trip to the station.

Ethan and Mattie manage to keep up a conversation as they drive through places reminiscent of experiences they had shared together. Ethan obliquely tries to tell Mattie of his shattered desire of running away with her, and Mattie then produces the letter to Zeena she had taken from Ethan's study. To make this scene dramatically important, Mrs. Wharton made no mention of what Mattie was doing in the study. Now the importance of Mattie's knowledge of Ethan's love becomes clear: she too realizes that breaking away from their environment is impossible, and up to this point and beyond, Mattie is stoically prepared to be separated from Ethan. Only as their time together draws ever shorter do the lovers entertain the idea of suicide.

As well, we find, Mrs. Wharton's scattered hints at Mattie's dreamy personality are confirmed. She, like Ethan, could build fantasies of love. While she is a happier and livelier person than Ethan, she is just as much of a "granite outcropping" in that she has scrupulously kept hidden her affection for him. Now all Ethan's fancies and imaginings of Mattie's unvoiced efforts at communication are proven to be correct. Moreover, all of Ethan's attempts at making his feelings known to Mattie probably were sensed and dreamed about by the girl ever since the summer day at Shadow Pond.

The wonder Ethan and Mattie feel at confirming that their imagined love for each other is indeed real is made sad by thoughts of their parting. Mrs. Wharton structures the journey up to and beyond this point like a piece of music in which joy and sadness alternate. The joy of returning to Shadow Pond precedes the sad necessity of continuing the journey; the joy of finding that love is shared precedes the sad realization that the love cannot be preserved. Here the first intimation of death as the destination appears in the thoughts of Ethan. And Mattie confirms Ethan's thought by wishing that she were dead.

After Ethan and Mattie have passed through Starkfield to the Corbury road, they arrive at the sledding hill, and here they decide to go sledding. Once again a kind of joy dominates the mood as the two enjoy the thrill of the first ride down the hill. Afterward, Ethan asks Mattie if she was scared of running into the elm tree. The reappearance of the idea of fear signals the mounting pressure of the death-wish building in the two lovers. As well, it echoes the portents of the sledding smashup which have been steadily increasing since the beginning of the book.

Now the discussion foreshadows the actual circumstances of the disaster in terms of Ethan's ability to steer a sled, a motif also repeated throughout the book. Ethan's steering connotes the feeling of masculinity in his relation with Mattie and his dominance and protection of her. His rightful masculine role, denied in his marriage to Zeena, is also connoted in Mattie's statement that Ethan has keen vision. Mrs. Wharton has carefully built up Ethan's powers of observation, beginning with his sensitivity to natural beauty and his conversations with Mattie in which he pointed out the stars and the features of the landscape. We should also be reminded of the role Ethan's sharp eyesight played in finding Mattie's locket.

As the themes of a powerful symphony are drawn together and restated at the finish, so does Mrs. Wharton bring together all the major themes of the novel. After the conversation about fear and the thrilling exaltation of the sled ride have passed, silence, darkness, and cold are emphasized as the lovers remount the hill. Ethan thinks that this will be their last walk together, and the thought portends not only the coming smashup, but also Mattie's future state as a cripple.

Another motif associated with the love of Ethan and Mattie is fulfilled now: since the walk home from the dance there has been a spot under the Varnum spruces associated with the lovers. There Ethan caught up with Mattie after she had refused a ride with Denis Eady. There Ethan saw Ned Hale and Ruth Varnum kissing, and later made a point of relating the incident to Mattie. Now this is the appropriate spot for a "goodbye" kiss.

Both Ethan and Mattie do not wish to be separated, and as the town clock strikes five, Mattie is seized with the idea of sledding down the Corbury hill to a mutual death. As Mattie tries to persuade him and then breaks into tears, Ethan's thoughts are a wild whirl of love for Mattie and rejection of Zeena. He wonders to himself what death will be like, and decides in ironic ignorance of his fate that he will feel nothing.

The sorrel's whinny, like a solo instrument in an orchestra, briefly reminds Ethan of his duties on the farm. Mattie's command, "Come," interrupts Ethan's thoughts; as Mrs. Wharton makes evident, Mattie has become the personification of Ethan's fate in that she urges him on when he might otherwise hold back and reconsider. We should also recall that before now Ethan was the one who commanded "Come along."

Once on the sled, however, Ethan resumes his role as the male authority. He tells Mattie to switch places with him so he will be in the front of the sled. His thoughts are confused before they push off down the hill but he convinces himself that Mattie was right, and they start as the sorrel whinnies again. As they near the elm Ethan has an ugly vision of Zeena's face which causes him to swerve the sled; but he resumes the course and steers the sled into the elm tree.

Mrs. Wharton next uses the effective device of describing Ethan's sense impressions as consciousness returns. First comes his sharp vision, and Ethan finds himself trying to determine if the star he sees is Sirius. Next, his hearing returns and with it the sound of a small animal calling out in pain. Then his sense of touch informs him that the sound comes from under his hand. Finally he realizes the awful fact that his arm has fallen across Mattie's face. As Mattie pronounces his name he also hears the whinny of the sorrel, which reminds him that he should be getting the horse its feed ration.

This dramatic sequence embodies the tableau of two destroyed lives with a tragic poignancy and calm. Mrs. Wharton does not tell us that the attempt at death has failed and that Ethan and Mattie are condemned to live out their crippled lives in Starkfield. Instead we sense with Ethan the quiet acceptance of his fate when he thinks that it is time to feed the sorrel. There can be no escape.

## IMAGERY, SYMBOLISM, STYLE

As suggested earlier in this commentary it may be helpful to compare the experience of reading this novel with that of hearing a piece of music. The major action and the development of theme can be seen as similar to a melody which can express feelings such as happiness, sadness, uncertainty, or determination. The patterns and sequences of imagery and symbolism in *Ethan Frome* might likewise be compared to the repeated yet varied musical motifs which enhance the main development of a piece of music. We have already dealt with these patterns and sequences in our discussion of the prologue and part one; we will find that the motifs of winter and summer, sickness and death, and silence and isolation are repeated and filled out in part two. We will also observe that Mrs. Wharton's spare prose builds and integrates the elements and levels of the novel to a compact yet complex climax in the events of chapter nine.

The imagery associated with Mattie in part two continues to be that of warmth, life, and the spring and summer. On the morning after their idyllic evening, Ethan notices that the humidity in the kitchen has made Mattie's hair especially curly so that it resembles the "traveller's joy," a climbing vine also appropriately known as "virgin's bowers."

We should recall that two other vines have figured in the imagery, but they were associated with death. In the prologue the narrator saw a black creeper on the Frome front porch; on the walk home with Mattie, Ethan observed a dead cucumber vine on the front porch. In these instances, the imagery of winter and death is coupled with the vision of the house twenty years after the tragedy and with the idea of a funeral crape for Zeena. Also appropriate to Zeena is the darkness which surrounds her during the confrontation of husband and wife after her return from Bettsbridge.

Within the space of two pages at the beginning of chapter seven, Mrs. Wharton uses these words to set the appropriate scene for action and idea: "dark," "obscurity," "dim," "twilight," and "darkness." As we have found, Mrs. Wharton is not one to heedlessly scatter modifiers and descriptive words; her purpose is to associate the events in the bedroom with a gloomy darkness appropriate to the effect of the argument on Ethan and Mattie. This same imagistic use of darkness later returns in a somewhat different context when the lovers are sledding on the Corbury road.

Except for the comparison of the combatants to venomous snakes, the description of the argument is nearly bare of other imagery than that of darkness. But when Ethan goes downstairs to eat dinner and reveals to Mattie that there has been trouble, imagery abounds. Mattie's fright causes her eyelashes to beat against Ethan's cheek "like netted butterflies." Ethan speaks to Mattie "as if he saw her drowning in a dream." Their conversation has the effect of "a torch of warning" in a "black landscape." Ethan feels as intoxicated as he does when kissing Mattie, but at the same time he is "dying of thirst for her lips."

These images are more ominous and suggestive of captivity and death than those previously associated with the lovers. Mrs. Wharton uses the images to heighten the mood of anxiety and to portend again the tragic end destined for the lovers. The smashup is also foreshadowed in Mrs. Wharton's description of Zeena carrying the pieces of the broken pickle dish "as if she carried a dead body." Ironically, Zeena's concern will soon have to be for the smashed and broken bodies of Ethan and Mattie.

Another object with symbolic overtones appears during Ethan's night in the study; while trying to make himself comfortable on his sofa he feels something hard against his cheek. It turns out to be the only piece of needlework Zeena had ever done, a cushion. Compared to Mattie, who enjoys such needlework as trimming hats, Zeena lacks femininity: she is too busy worrying over her ills. That Ethan throws Zeena's cushion aside is symbolic of his growing rejection of her and prepares us for Ethan's thoughts of running away to the West with Mattie.

But Ethan's dream of escape is impossible; Mrs. Wharton uses another image of captivity, "prison-warders handcuffing a convict," to convey the feeling of despair which seeps into Ethan. He is caught in physical and mental darkness, his only gleam of hope all but snuffed out. At this point Mrs. Wharton uses her powers of description to the full to contrast Ethan's gloom with a sudden, mocking illumination of the night sky as the "pure moon" reveals all the natural beauty of the landscape that Ethan associates with Mattie.

As Ethan walks toward Andrew Hale's the next morning, the imagery of nature appears again. Preparing for Ethan and

Mattie's afternoon ride, Mrs. Wharton stresses that there is a hint of spring on this beautiful day. Everything he passes seems to Ethan to be related to some memory of Mattie, and a birdcall he hears reminds him of Mattie's laughter. The feelings of happiness and hope aroused in Ethan by the spring day are soon to be quashed when he decides that he cannot ask the Hales for money.

We should note that the description of the spring weather comprises one paragraph of condensed prose; this method of writing is one of Mrs. Wharton's ways of drawing deliberate attention to the relation of natural beauty to Ethan's sense of meanings. While he found the appearance of the moon the night before a mocking contrast to his despairing state, the next morning Ethan is heartened by a suggestion of spring in the atmosphere and the reminders of Mattie it brings.

Prevented by his own conscience from attempting to get money from the Hales, and angered by Zeena's callous treatment of Mattie in asking her to bring her own trunk downstairs, Ethan's feelings are at a low point when he finds Mattie in her room crying because she thought he had deserted her. The warmth Ethan generates by comforting her is described in his perception of her hair. Ethan finds Mattie's hair one of her most beautiful features; it is symbolic of her free, happy, and open personality. Zeena's hair, on the other hand, is always unattractively crimped and confined with pins just as her personality seems pinched and constrained. The symbolic use of Mattie's hair grows more important at the climax of the novel, when it represents for Ethan the beauty and love that he wants to give his love for.

The most important section of sustained imagistic prose in *Ethan Frome* occurs during the second half of chapter nine. It is on the journey to the station by way of Shadow Pond that the true extent of their mutual love is first revealed to Ethan and Mattie. Appropriate to this discovery, the imagery describing the surroundings, memories, and feelings of the lovers is warm, nostalgic, and melancholy. We have already discussed how the name "Shadow Pond" evokes some of the feeling of the scene which is set there.

The descriptions of the drive to the pond and the pond itself are rich with images of natural beauty. This kind of description is not characteristic of the rest of the novel; because the setting for most of *Ethan Frome* is stark and cold, we should be especially struck by the obvious pains Mrs. Wharton has taken to make the scene at Shadow Pond especially beautiful and meaningful to the lovers. There they recall the church picnic the summer before where Mattie had lost her locket and Ethan had found it.

The incident brought a special happiness like that of surprising "a butterfly in the winter woods." Just as we discovered different significant usages of the imagery of vines, we find the same to be true of butterflies. Here, the butterfly of the image is especially notable because it has defied the cold and death of winter and has preserved its beauty alone and free. The "netted butterflies" which were used to describe Mattie's eyelashes blinking away tears evoke the captivity of the lovers under the powerful rule of Zeena.

The description of Shadow Pond and of Ethan and Mattie grows more melancholy as twilight approaches and with it the time that she must be delivered to the train station. Ethan is again attracted to Mattie's hair and its odor of the woods, but he cannot bring himself to tell her his feelings, and silence once more dominates the two as they leave Shadow Pond. Increasing darkness prevails over the imagery as Ethan and Mattie approach their crippling accident.

Mrs. Wharton ominously suggests the mood of the tragic climax and the characters' thoughts of death when she has the darkness come "dropping down like a black veil from the heavy hemlock boughs." The black veil may remind us of a funeral and the hemlock of poison. In the same vein, the Varnum spruces seem to be a "black curtain," and the elm tree on the sledding run seems to have a "deadly elbow" on the first ride downhill. Just before Mattie urges Ethan to ride the sled a second time it seems to him that the darkness and silence under the Varnum spruces is like being buried in a coffin.

As the idea of sledding to a mutual death gains momentum, Ethan is caught in a frenzy of love for Mattie which blots out all his former conscientious thoughts of not leaving Zeena to fend for herself. Ethan is overwhelmed by the knowledge that Mattie has indeed loved him. Ethan's ecstasy is now associated with Mattie's hair and with summer warmth at Shadow Pond. Only the touch of Mattie's cold cheek and the whistle of the approaching train bring him out of his vision.

But the whole idea of mutual suicide now is identified in Ethan's mind as a sort of quest to preserve the love and beauty of his relationship with Mattie; he does not consider the alternatives as he had the night in the study or on the road to the Hales. Passion, not reason, dominates his mind; appropriately, the darkness has increased and his usually sharp vision is dimmed, just as his rational faculties are dimmed in the obscurity of passion.

As they coast downhill, the last thing Ethan sees before the tree is a spectral vision of his wife's face, a manifestation of his conception of her as an alien presence. It seems to try to prevent him from attaining the goal of the tree, but he maneuvers around it. The vision is a symbolic reminder to us that Ethan will never escape Zeena's dominance, that he will fail tragically in his attempt to carry away in death the beauty and love he had found with Mattie.

After the crash, Mrs. Wharton's prose tells us what Ethan feels and sees; he had wondered briefly what it would be like after death but now he slowly realizes he is still alive. Mattie seems to him a small, soft animal crying in agony; then he realizes he is touching her hair and face. The seed of beauty he had tried to find stroking her hair before the smashup has turned into the twisted, ugly reality which he will have to bear for the many years until his death.

As we have seen, the careful prose style Mrs. Wharton uses is remarkably appropriate to the characters and theme of the story. As *Ethan Frome* moves to its climax we are more than ever able to appreciate the art with which the story is fashioned. In thinking of Mrs. Wharton's prose style we should recall how much connotative power it has. Its elliptical and stark surface conceals a wealth of meaning, as she hinted in her Introduction to the novel. Her art, like the emblematic granite outcropping, is mostly hidden beneath the surface.

## THE EPILOGUE

The epilogue begins at the point in time when, more than twenty years after the tragedy, the narrator suspended the prologue to give us his vision of the story of Ethan Frome. The epilogue is a *denouement*, or final unraveling of the plot of the main story and the frame tale. As well, it gives us the finishing touches of irony and tragic poignancy.

As he enters the room, the "querulous drone" the narrator had heard outside the door stops, and Mrs. Wharton suspends the identification of the speaker until after she has described the effects of twenty years and the smashup on Zeena and Mattie. It is Mattie who has spoken, the narrator learns, when she begins to complain about Zeena having fallen asleep and let the room get cold. There is no need at this point for further details of the narrator's stay at the farm; the irony of reversal here is best when simply stated. Mattie has lost her sweet temperament and now deserves the word "querulous," used often in the body of the novel in association with Zeena. Zeena, on the other hand, has had to take on the full household duties and the care of two invalids.

The epilogue continues as the narrator tells of his conversation with Mrs. Ned Hale the evening of his return from the Frome farm. Mrs. Hale is somewhat surprised that Ethan had taken the narrator in for the night; she and the doctor are the only visitors usually admitted. Mrs. Hale makes the trip now only about twice a year, and she prefers to go when she knows Ethan will not be home because she can sense the terrible pain he feels at being trapped in the cold, bare farmhouse.

The narrator is fishing for information from Mrs. Hale, and he tries to win her confidence so that she may add something to what he already knows of the story. She says that after the accident Mattie was taken to the Varnum house, and when she regained consciousness she confided in Mrs. Hale (who was then Ruth Varnum) the truth about the sledding accident. Mrs. Hale has never been able to find out what Zeena thought of the accident, but she finds it miraculous that Zeena was able to assume the responsibility of caring for Ethan and Mattie for so many years. Zeena has never changed from her sickliness, but she has put aside her imagined illnesses and her overdeveloped sense of self-pity. Mrs. Hale's explanation for Mattie's change of temperament is that she has undergone too much suffering. But she thinks it is Ethan who has suffered most, especially since Mattie was not killed in the mishap.

As Mrs. Hale suggests, Ethan, the most introspective and sensitive of the characters, has suffered a life in death after the smashup. The repeated graveyard image is ironic because Ethan had twice dreamily speculated about his life in connection with the Frome graveyard. The first time he thought of himself as living out his years with Mattie, the second time of enduring his life with Zeena. He did not suspect his fate was to be a nightmarish combination of the two daydreams.

Cold now dominates the Frome farm, stripped of its "L"; many of the comforts of the house are gone, sold, we may suppose, to keep the three alive. The once-productive sawmill now is an "exanimate" ruin, and the fields are starved and sterile. And Ethan, we should recall, is a scarred and disfigured cripple, aged fifty-two years. To fully comprehend the unrelieved bitterness of the tragedy, one should reread the prologue.

# Notes on the Main Characters

## ETHAN FROME

Tall, lean, and powerful with blue eyes and blond hair, Ethan attracts the narrator's attention as "the most striking figure in Starkfield" even after the disfiguration caused by the smashup. As a young man, Ethan is sensitive, intelligent, and imaginative; an interrupted and incomplete college education stimulates his mind to an awareness that perceived reality conceals deep significances. Yearning to escape the parochial environment of Starkfield, Ethan is frustrated by the necessity of caring for his ailing mother and for the family farm. To combat the silence, isolation, and loneliness of life, Ethan marries Zenobia Pierce after his mother's death. Because she will not leave Starkfield and because she develops into an oppressively silent hypochrondriac, Ethan is still unable to break away from the laborious captivity of his farm.

When Mattie Silver arrives to help out with the household duties, Ethan finds a kindred spirit, and over the course of a year he falls in love with her. Mattie's presence fills Ethan with dreams of happiness which are sharp contrasts to the appalling actuality of Zeena. Convinced that he could live happily with Mattie, and humiliated and repulsed by Zeena's conniving dominance of his life, Ethan plans to run off with his wife's young cousin. The plan cannot be put into action, and in order to preserve the happiness and beauty of their love, Ethan and Mattie abandon themselves to the emotion of the moment and make an abortive attempt at suicide which leaves them crippled for life.

Ethan is named after Ethan the Ezrahite of I Kings 4:31 in the Old Testament. In Hebrew, his name connotes strength, firmness, and permanence, and all these qualities apply directly and ironically to Ethan Frome's character. A physically powerful man, Ethan nevertheless is dominated by Zeena. The very mention of her name causes fear and instead of being firm with her, Ethan is deceitful or submissive. As for permanence, Ethan's noblest quality is the stoic endurance of his tragedy. There is no hope for Ethan; the moral landscape of Starkfield offers no redemption and no new life. *Ethan Frome* is not a Christian novel and there is no power greater than man to offer mercy or salvation or even pity.

Ethan must live out his days surrounded by the elements of a harsh and indifferent nature: there may be beauty and warmth in the spring and summer, but the winters come again every year and with them new hardships to endure. For Ethan the only escape from the cold, the silence, the isolation, and the loneliness of his life is a headstone in the Frome' graveyard. Ethan's own realization of his situation is what causes his great mental anguish. At the beginning of the novel the narrator catches only a glimpse of Ethan's face at an unguarded moment, but it is enough to cause him to cry out "He looks as if he was dead and in hell now!"

## ZENOBIA (ZEENA) FROME

Except for brief hints from other characters in the frame sections, what we know of Zeena's character comes from Ethan's memory and from the action of the main story. Seven years older than Ethan (she is thirty-five at the beginning of the main story), Zeena is portrayed as old before her time. Mrs. Wharton is quite unflattering in her descriptions of Zeena, who is gaunt, sallow-faced, and wrinkled. She has false teeth and she wears her hair severely pulled back with crimping pins. She is flat-chested, asthmatic, and thoroughly unfeminine; she speaks in a plaintive, whiny drawl. Ethan was twenty-one and Zeena twenty-eight when they were married; it is only charity to suppose that what beauty she might have had was in its last bloom and fading fast. And it is no wonder that Ethan is attracted to Mattie.

Zeena's name is appropriately reminiscent of the famous Queen Zenobia of Palmyra (third century A.D.), who ruled a city-state which for a short time defied the Roman Empire. Even when captured she was too much for her (male) conquerors; she persuaded them to give her a triumphal procession in Rome and substantial possessions near Tivoli. While Zeena lacks the power and beauty of Queen Zenobia, she is nevertheless monarch over the Frome household. During seven years of marriage she has enforced her will on Ethan by all the conniving means in her power.

Ethan knew that he could not move away from Starkfield because Zeena did not want to live in a city where she would have no identity. Her hypochondria and her few legitimate illnesses have served as excuses for her to indulge in patent remedies and expensive visits to doctors at a time when Ethan was struggling to pay off the heavy mortgage on the farm and still maintain financial solvency. More important, however, she uses her illness to enforce her decision that Mattie must go and a hired housekeeper must come to take her place.

Under such a powerful rule Ethan has reason to think of his wife as a "mysterious alien presence" and an "evil energy." Zeena is silent, secretive, and observant. When she does speak it is to voice either a want or a criticism; consequently, before the arrival of Mattie silence had prevailed in the Frome household. There never was and never would be any real communication between Ethan and his wife. Ethan's imagination about Zeena is so powerful that he fancies she knows his innermost thoughts. The extent of her authority is such that Ethan and Mattie are both uneasy when reminded of her; Mattie cannot even sit comfortably in Zeena's rocking chair while Zeena is in Bettsbridge. Ethan's last impression before the sled hits the elm tree is that he sees a horribly disfigured specter of Zeena's face.

But despite all her undesirable qualities, Zeena also responds to the tragedy with stoic endurance as she takes the responsibility for the care of Ethan and Mattie. She never says what she thinks of the smashup, her querulousness continues, but she is finally drawn out of her hypochondriac self-indulgence by the need to minister to others.

## MATTIE SILVER

Mattie's last name is suggestive not only of how precious she becomes to Ethan but also of the role money plays as one of the determinants of the fate of the two lovers. Because Zeena thinks Ethan will be paid a fifty-dollar advance she hires a girl to take Mattie's place. Because Ethan cannot bring himself to pressure Andrew Hale for the advance, he does not have enough money to run away with Mattie. Since they cannot escape alive, the two decide that their only alternative is to die together. Ironically, they escape death but are condemned to live out their crippled lives in absolute poverty.

We have already discussed at length the imagery associated with Mattie; we should remember that most of it is not directly imposed on her by Mrs. Wharton. Rather, the images usually are part of Ethan's thoughts about Mattie. The imagery not only describes her, it tells us in what terms Ethan thinks of her.

Perhaps the most important fact about Mattie is that she does indeed love Ethan, but this fact is not conclusively revealed to Ethan nor to us until after the two have left Shadow Pond on their way to the train. There are, of course, ample hints that Mattie likes Ethan and could be happy if married to him, but they are hints only. Although Ethan imagines that Mattie loves him, he cannot be absolutely sure. It is most appropriate to the development of the story that the depth of Mattie's love is not revealed until the climactic chapter. Neither Mattie nor Ethan seriously considers running away to become lovers until their evening idyll has proved them domestically compatible and until Zeena has forced the issue by insisting that Mattie go back to Stamford. Even then, Ethan's decision not to desert Zeena or deceive the Hales precludes running away.

It is only when Ethan finds out the true extent of Mattie's love that he can be swayed by passion into thoughts of suicide. Instead of fancied hints of affection to daydream about, Ethan is given conclusive proof of Mattie's love. The two are enveloped in a surge of passion which sweeps them along to their ruin. If they had stopped to reason, Ethan and Mattie could have preserved themselves and their love — Ethan could have waited the three months until Andrew Hale paid off his $300 and then gone to Stamford to fetch Mattie and run away to the West.

Finally, we should note the status of Mattie after the smash-up is the cruelest irony that Ethan has to endure. She is no more than a vegetable with the power of speech. As Mrs. Ned Hale points out, if Mattie had died there would have been some hope that Ethan might have lived. But because Ethan has had to exist for twenty years with the horribly deformed remains of a once beautiful, sensitive, and loving girl, he has had to surrender himself to the forces of isolation, silence, darkness, cold, and death in life.

# Motifs

## SILENCE

In *Ethan Frome* each of the three major characters is encased in his own silence. Ethan, a quiet man by nature, asks his cousin Zeena to marry him so that he will not have to spend a lonely and silent winter on the farm. Zeena grows silent after their marriage and forces a smothering silence on Ethan and later on Mattie. The silence of the characters is symbolic of their inability to communicate with one another in order to dispel their own loneliness. Ethan and Mattie slowly break this silence and find joy and love in sharing their thoughts and feelings with each other. But in the maelstrom of emotion generated by the necessity of parting at the very time when their communication is the deepest (that is, when they realize the extent of their love for each other), they abandon rational thought and cast themselves downhill into a silent hell in which the only sounds come from the two complaining women.

## ISOLATION

The motif of silence is complementary to the motif of isolation of man from his fellow men. The isolation of the characters before the tragedy is not self-imposed, but is enforced upon them by outside circumstances. Ethan tried to escape the isolation of Starkfield and his father's farm by going off to the technological college at Worcester. While he became aware of the physical forces working in the universe and began to overcome his reticence and to cultivate his own social traits, his father's death forced him to give up college and return to the farm and his ailing mother. After his marriage to Zeena, Ethan was tied even closer to the stark farm where he had grown up; in effect, he was isolated physically from the world at large and he is also cut off from the possibility of any human fellowship that life in a village might afford.

With the arrival of Mattie, Ethan finds a kindred spirit. Isolated from her past by the deaths of both parents and the ill will of most of her relatives, she is plunged into an unfamiliar farmhouse and, except for church socials, is cut off from contact with human beings other than the Fromes. When Ethan and Mattie begin to communicate, they begin to break out of their isolation as well as their silence. The attempted escape fails tragically, however, and Ethan, Mattie, and Zeena are left to spend their lives in an isolation even more complete than that from which they tried to flee.

# ILLUSION VERSUS REALITY

Each of the three main characters in *Ethan Frome* finds some means of escaping the reality of silence and isolation through illusion. Before real communication takes place, Ethan and Mattie both dream of loving the other. Their illusions are, in a sense, healthy; there is some basis for them in reality, and until the tragic climax the fantasies of love become less illusory and more real. Their respective dream worlds of the joy of love are proven possible by their experience of the evening without Zeena.

Zeena's illusions, appropriately, are unhealthy. Her hypochondria enables her to escape into self-pity and self-indulgence; before the smashup forces her to abandon her illusions she is about to escape from all her household responsibilities through the device of a hired housekeeper. Mrs. Wharton's fine sense of tragic irony works to make Zeena the only one who in any way is changed for the good by the tragedy: she is forced to minister to her husband and cousin and has neither the time nor the money to indulge her sickly tendencies.

# Style

In her Introduction to *Ethan Frome* Mrs. Wharton states that the theme of the novel "must be treated as starkly and summarily as life had always presented itself to my protagonists. . . ." She follows her own prescription throughout the book; her style is characterized by a simplicity and sometimes even a barrenness appropriate to the stark and tragic quality of the whole story. Mrs. Wharton is always careful to choose vocabulary and sentence structure peculiarly suited to the situation she is treating. Her apparent surface simplicity can be deceptive, especially late in the novel when she has built up patterns of imagery, patterns of behavior, and specially charged words.

If Mrs. Wharton's descriptions seem at first almost elliptical or incomplete it is because she does not indulge herself with superfluous or merely decorative modifiers. Adjectives and adverbs stand out because they are used infrequently; and, when they are used, they are well chosen. Her imagery is always appropriate to the limitations of her characters — she does not describe them in words they would not be able to understand themselves. She draws most often upon elemental nature: stars, heat, cold, the seasons, animals, vegetation, light, darkness. These are the things most familiar to the reticent and inarticulate New Englanders she portrays.

One of the best examples of Mrs. Wharton's careful control of her style is seen in her description of the events immediately before and after the sled crash. As Mattie and Ethan ride their sled down the hill, Mrs. Wharton captures the initial thrill of the speed and then Ethan's frenzied determination to drive them straight into the elm. Then her prose becomes slow and spare in order to evoke Ethan's return to consciousness. Not only in this example, but everywhere in the novel her style is restrained, so that the way the words are arranged enhances their meaning without calling attention to the cleverness of the arrangement.

# Review Questions and Theme Topics

1. In her Introduction Mrs. Wharton calls *Ethan Frome* a "tragedy." What justification is there for this label? Can Ethan be seen as a tragic hero with a flaw who is responsible for the terrible catastrophe?

2. Mrs. Wharton also says that the theme of *Ethan Frome* "must be treated as starkly and summarily as life had always presented itself to my protagonists. . . ." How does Mrs. Wharton's prose style accomplish her goal? How are the imagery and setting of the novel related to this idea of presentation?

3. In discussing the structure of *Ethan Frome* Mrs. Wharton says that Harmon Gow and Mrs. Ned Hale contribute to the narrative *"just so much as he or she is capable of understanding. . . ."* Judging from the prologue, comment on the personal limitations of these two characters insofar as these limitations affect what they contribute to the narrative.

4. One of the devices responsible for the tightly knit structure of *Ethan Frome* is foreshadowing. How does Mrs. Wharton employ this device to prepare the reader for the smashup? Zeena is the last major character to be directly introduced into the story; how does Mrs. Wharton prepare the reader to meet Zeena?

5. In the prologue and epilogue a narrator-character tells us the story. What limitations are there on what he does and does not know? Why is it necessary for Mrs. Wharton to switch to omniscient narration for the body of the novel?

6. The omniscient narration of the body of the novel focuses almost entirely on the experiences of Ethan as the means of relating the action. What limitations are there on what the reader learns because of this device. Where does Mrs.

Wharton occasionally drop this device to analyze Ethan's experiences for us? What is accomplished in each instance?

7. Repetitive patterns of imagery are an important part of *Ethan Frome*. What are some of these repetitive patterns or sequences? How do they help us interpret character and action? How are they associated with the motifs of silence, isolation, and illusion versus reality?

8. *Ethan Frome* lends itself to interpretation as (a) a deterministic tragedy of circumstances in which the characters had no control over their destiny or (b) a tragedy of error in which the characters had control over their destiny and could have averted it had errors of judgment or the usurpation of reason by passion not occurred. Choose one of these positions and show why you agree with it by citing examples from the novel which support your choice; in addition, defend your choice by advancing arguments which show the other interpretation to be invalid.

9. An important structural device in *Ethan Frome* is that of parallel. Discuss the significant similarities in the following paralleled situations: (a) Zeena's appearance on the back porch the night of the dance and Mattie's appearance the following night; (b) Ethan's thoughts about the Frome graveyard on the same two nights.

10. The three most important women in Ethan's life are associated with sickness. Discuss Ethan's attitudes toward the sicknesses of his mother, his wife, and Mattie. What do Ethan's attitudes show about the effect these illnesses have on his character?

11. From the evidence of the novel itself, defend one of these two points of view: (a) *Ethan Frome* is a novel of hope; (b) *Ethan Frome* is a novel of despair.

12. Why does Mrs. Wharton attempt to reproduce the New England dialect of some of the characters? What is the effect

on the reader of the difference between the standard English diction of the narration and the dialect of the characters?

13. Mrs. Wharton is extremely careful to pick just the right word to give a particular shading or tone to her descriptive prose. Choose a scene of descriptive prose (not conversation) and analyze the use of vocabulary. Is the vocabulary appropriate to Mrs. Wharton's stated purpose of stark and summary presentation? What sorts of adjectives and adverbs are present? Are any words superfluous or simply decorative?

14. Suppose the main body of the novel was focused through Zeena's mind instead of Ethan's. In what ways would this change your sympathies with the characters? Speculate on what Zeena thinks of the smashup and its twenty-year aftermath.

15. Discuss the function of money in the novel.

16. For research outside the novel: Discuss *Ethan Frome* as example of *naturalistic* fiction or as an example of *regionalistic* fiction.

17. Comment briefly on the significance of each of the following: (a) the pickle dish, (b) Ethan's unfinished letter to Zeena, (c) Mattie's hair, (d) the "L", (e) Zeena's cat, (f) the "cushion" Zeena made for Ethan, (g) Mattie's locket, (h) the sorrel's whinnying, (i) the "exanimate" sawmill, (j) the narrator's book of popular science.

18. Analyze the development of Ethan and Mattie's love for each other. What are the similar and different traits of character which attract them to each other? Discuss the role of illusion versus reality in their growing love.

19. Discuss the narrator's comment that Ethan lived "in a depth of moral isolation." Does the narrator mean that Ethan is isolated from morality or that he is moral but isolated?

# Selected Bibliography

HOWE, IRVING (ed.). *Edith Wharton: A Collection of Critical Essays*. New York: Prentice-Hall, 1962. Two of the essays deal specifically with *Ethan Frome;* some others touch on it.

KELLOGG, GRACE. *The Two Lives of Edith Wharton: The Woman and Her Work*. New York: Appleton Century Crofts, 1965. This biography is concerned far more with the woman than with her work.

NEVIUS, BLAKE. *Edith Wharton: A Study of Her Fiction*. Berkeley: University of California Press, 1953. The best critical study of Mrs. Wharton's work, it includes penetrating observations on *Ethan Frome*. Selections collected in the Howe book.

THOMAS, J. D. "Marginalia on Ethan Frome," *American Literature*, XXVII (November, 1955), 405-09. Thomas objects to the way Mrs. Wharton handles the "moral crisis" when Ethan decides he should not seek money from the Hales.

TRILLING, LIONEL. "The Morality of Inertia," *Great Moral Dilemmas*. New York: Harper & Row, 1956. Reprinted in Howe. Trilling claims that there is no moral decision in *Ethan Frome*.

WHARTON, EDITH. *A Backward Glance*. New York: Appleton Century Crofts, 1934. Autobiographical reminiscenses, a few of which touch upon the background to *Ethan Frome*.

_____. *"The Writing of Ethan Frome,"* Colophon, Pt. 2 (1931), pp. 1-4. Mrs. Wharton describes the origin of the novel as an exercise for her French instructor.

# ETHAN FROME GENEALOGY

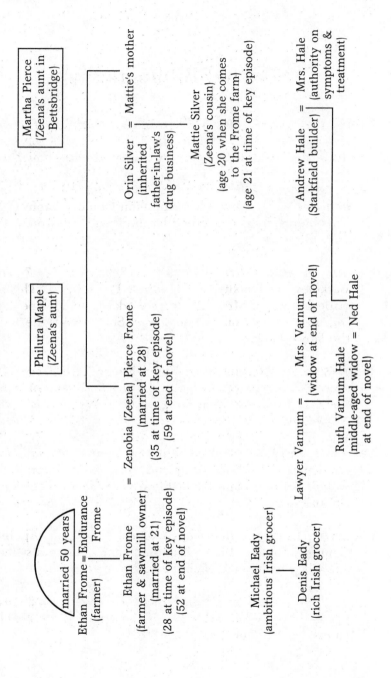

# NOTES

# NOTES

# NOTES

# NOTES

NOTES